Chapter 1

Get To Know Me

Hi, I'm Amie a 26 year old girl with autism from Swansea. I was diagnosed with autism at the age of 6 years old. I grew up in Swansea with my mum and my big family. I'd always be at my Auntie Catherine's and be doing tumble tosses in the living room, yeah that's me, crazy from the start. I even remember being in the old house in the back garden jumping chair to chair, as to me it was fun and falling in between, ouch! I did the weirdest things. No, I couldn't do them now, as in the tumble tosses. Then I had a sister called Mia when I was 8, and a brother called Lewis when I was 10. Lewis was on my dad's side as my mum and dad are not together, so me and my brother have different mums and me and my sister have different
dads I loved being a big sister to them.

My mum Claire, noticed I acted different to other kids but I was always a happy child I loved singing, playing with dolls and just being crazy. I was always fussy with food only eating nuggets, sausage, chips and potato apart from all the junk food. I had my friends in school, but it was always hard for me to mix with other kids. I liked to have my photo taken and I would pull weird faces. I had my tantrums and was a quiet child at the same time.
Apparently, I was the little angel as my Nanny Sooty said. Are you sure about that?

My family has always said, as I got older that I'm too nice a person and that's why ex friends used me. Probably why I didn't have many friends. My friends were my dolls that I loved to play with.

When I started to grow up, I still loved my dolls. I loved to sing and just be myself. I loved toys but still didn't mix well with other people my age. I hung out more with my cousins as we were close. When we would all go out with my Nanny Sooty and my Grampa Sooty, we would nag to sleep over there together. This is my nanny on my dad's side.

I never grew up like others my age I've always been a little childish. My family think I'm crazy but caring and kind I was shy at times. I always enjoyed being around family, going out and staying over both my nanny's houses.

Pink has always been my favourite colour. I've been obsessed with music my whole life, always one song at a time repeating it over and over.

I get attached to certain people when they make an effort to understand me and come into my bubble or my world.

All my family especially my mum has always supported me through it all even when things got hard.

Becoming a teenager was a difficult time for me. My body changing, it was scary becoming a woman. I only had one friend at a time in school. Most of the time the one friend I had never lasted long. Maybe because I didn't communicate very well, sometimes the friends I would meet would be very similar to me. The same difficulties and challenges.

By this point I loved Bratz dolls, they were the only thing I liked playing. I think I was obsessed with them.

Still the same with Music.

But this time I started trying more foods, nothing green though, just like fish and real meats, proper chicken and beef. Also, swede which I happened to love and didn't stop eating it, which was a shock to myself after years of being fussy. The best thing I ever did was to get obsessed with Avril Lavigne, her music was awesome, so of course I got attached to the colours dark pink and black. I still love those colours today.

It was about the age 13 that I started writing stories, funny ones though, not ones like this. I even put my teachers in them ha-ha! I typed so many that it helped me learn how to spell and write properly and not messy. When I got to comprehensive school, I attended the STF (special teaching facility). I would sit in the chill out area in school at break time or whenever I had free time and just write. I had a friend at this point who I was close to, sometimes she would sit with me and we would laugh as I'd write. I now look back and feel happy about those times. Even when I got home, I'd still write! That's basically what I did all the time apart from listen to music but it's what I loved doing and it's what kept me happy. I felt relaxed in my own little world. But then again being able to write or type a book and then publish it had been my dream. It's the only thing I wanted to be apart from a Rockstar ha-ha!!

Another thing I was obsessed with was being a Rockstar, I always called Avril Lavigne a Rockstar which she is, but where we live, we say musician, but not to me. In my head anyone like her is a Rockstar!

Then I found this guy I fancied in school. This was a brand-new feeling to me. I never knew you could have feelings like that, I was only 13, I was so shy to tell him. He was also Autistic. I wanted to be old school, so I wrote him a letter and a week later he replied. He said yeah ok! I'll be honest I asked him out! He was only a year older than me so 14, we were both so young, but we lasted together 5 years, he was my first boyfriend. Things just didn't work out in the end, but it was nice to know how it felt to have a boyfriend. Being autistic doesn't ever stop you from dating or fancying someone you still have the same feelings as anyone would.

I thought I had a future with him, I like to imagine things before they happen. I know some people say don't plan, just go with the flow but I have a habit of planning my future.

I got attached to his mum she was a lovely lady we still keep in contact today.

Chapter 2

How Things Were At Home

My Past.

Things started getting stressful and scary at home. My ex-stepdad started making me feel scared and saying things like I was hard work because of my autism. But I still smiled, carried on writing my stories and listening to music as I would normally. I would keep my distance as much as I could and was too shy to talk. I just felt like if I didn't have autism, he would of liked me more, but who knows. I wanted to run away. My meltdowns got bad from frustration, I'd hit out or kick things even sometimes throw things depends how bad the meltdowns got. It was the worst time when I look back.

At this time a lady came into my life, my mums' friend, who I like to call my Auntie Ali. She really helped, she made me feel more calm and I wasn't scared when I was around her. I was still shy, but she still managed to talk to me, she understood my autism. After being bullied in school for years, why did he have to come into my life and bully me too! He would make that scary face at me, which I always said he was a much scarier version of the Hulk. Me, my mum and my sister would end up arguing and I felt frustrated all the time. When I was around my Auntie Ali, at her house Id cry to not leave as I didn't want to go home. Me and my mum did get along a lot of the time and as I said she's the one person who's supported me. I hated having meltdowns at this point especially because I felt bad because I didn't want my little sister seeing me this way. But I knew I couldn't help it once one started it took hours for one to stop or for me to calm down.

Just the way I was treated by him made me feel anxious and I think that's where the anxiety started. There was an occasion where I was grounded, can't remember what for, there was a BQQ at Ali's and I wasn't allowed to go. That really started a meltdown, I ended up walking down there and sitting on the wall not far from her house. He tried to pick me up in the car to take me home, NO! I wasn't gonna get in the car with him as at this point. I was not happy; I was ready to blow! Ali had to get me in the car. Typing this is strange as it's been so long since this happened but it's part of my life. I was only ok around him when the whole family was around. I felt happier and more comfortable and I loved hanging out with my little cousins Faye & Adam. I would pretend I was going to Africa with Adam; we would pack our bags and get a tent and go out of my nanny's back garden. This is my family on my mums' side. We would go on to the wooden porch and get the tent up and pretend we saw tigers and other animals that you would see in Africa. Our favourite thing to do and I loved it, he was only about 6 and I was a young teenager.

We even would say to our mums "guess what? We saw tigers just now in Africa!" They must of thought we were losing our minds but we did explain that it was our imaginary game we did for fun.

This house that was our nanny's house that then became our house. I feel this is when the good and the bad started. You could say we moved a lot; I've lived in a few houses with my mum.

Big changes have always been hard for me. But the hardest was this past I had to go through. If I didn't have the big family I have, sticking by me and keeping me safe including my mum who's had to put up with all the meltdowns, having Ali in my life I don't know where I would be! I would of run away from my ex-Stepdad. I forgot to mention I say ex-stepdad because I don't like saying his name.

By the time I was 16 I had another little brother on my dad's side called Iwan. I was a big sister again for the 3rd time. He was so cute, and I loved him so much. I always looked after him and babysat him. As I was older now so could do more, he helped me with my autism, kept me calm.

There was one moment that scared me the most. When me and my sister had an argument, I ripped up paper that she had written on, I felt bad for doing it straight away. Ex-stepdad came in like a bull and went to slap me, but my auntie Catherine stopped him thank god. It took time but my mum left him. This was such a relief; he was kicked out of the house and it was just me and my sister for a few years. I was no longer scared or frustrated.

Time went by and my mum met another guy called Lee who is amazing this is when things started changing for the better, I started to calm down more. Yeah me and my sister still had our on/off sister arguments and me and my mum started to get along. I had other boyfriends which also didn't last, let's just say things happen for a reason. Being in that house now was lovely. My past started to go from scary to very relaxed. We did more family things; my mum even gave me two more sisters with Lee called Poppy and Maisy. I was so happy I even cried with joy. My new stepdad, Lee, had a nephew called Lewis who's now my cousin. We ended up not just family we ended up as best friends! We hung out every weekend had good times. Just when I thought I would never have a friend, he came along and today he's so supportive with everything. Ali was always there for for me she never fails to make me happy then and now but there was no crying leaving her home any More as I wanted to go home.

I was older now, a young adult, the bad past seemed to have gone. I still had bad memories of it, and it would upset me, but I was strong. Autism was always hard going through this. But I got through it with everyone around me. Just because you have autism you can still get through tough times.

Chapter 3

My Meltdowns.

How I Cope With Them.

I get meltdowns every time plans change, or something makes me frustrated. I get the worst meltdowns from crying to throwing things and banging my hands together or banging something. Sometimes I cannot control them and other time's I know how to somehow calm down. By sitting down taking deep breathes and sometimes I write what made it start in my diary. I mostly like being left a alone because if someone is trying to talk to me I get worse, I don't know what to do, it's hard to deal with them, but as you get older you find ways to calm yourself. I even have my salt lamp which I turn on every night.

I've had some pretty big ones through the years. One time I thought I broke my toe by kicking a chair, which wasn't clever! Or I've started swearing and shouting and it tends to happen to whoever is standing there and I feel terrible afterwards. In that moment I feel like my head is spinning, like the whole world is against me and that everyone is out to hate me, even though I know that's not the case. My worst one was swearing at my mum and Auntie Ali in a local pub. They had to take me outside and the worst part was where we were. I felt so ashamed, most meltdowns are out of the blue and I don't know why I have them. Sometimes it's when I don't want to do something because to me it's a big deal and I think at this moment I didn't want to leave the pub. I was having fun and when my mum said its time to leave it was the end of the world for me, I even scared myself in that moment as I didn't know how to stop myself from swearing and shouting.

I've also had a meltdown because I couldn't wear the shoe's I wanted. I tried to be a girlie girl for once by wearing high heel shoes, I couldn't actually walk in them, so my mum was telling me to change them, this was at a restaurant I think it was Christmas time. I started crying and shouting I couldn't understand why I couldn't walk in them, I threw one of the shoes and again I felt so bad, I did calm down and I did get over it and it ended up as a good time. I hate my meltdowns they make me feel so silly, but I know it's just my autism and I can't help it. I am glad I got mum who is patient with me and supports me no matter how big a meltdown is, and she forgives me afterwards. I will say the other family members are patient too. I've had a meltdown at my nanny Baileys house (this is my mums mum) where I was frustrated at something and threw my headphones on the floor and I cried for a little while but did calm down, my nan was very good with me.

I have a great family. I've also had meltdowns at my auntie Ali's house. I've sat on her stairs crying, I ripped up a letter! I don't remember why my mind goes funny and I can't think straight, and I had so many more I guess being autistic you have millions of meltdowns. Everyone is different as some are small and some are big, like the one I had where my mum took me to my Nanny Sooty's house I think it was to calm down, I just couldn't and was crying and banging my hands together. I left and started walking around the street, my mum did end up getting me back in the car and dropped me to my dad's house. I just couldn't stop crying but I went in and had some time with my little brothers it helped me calm down a lot. The worst part about having autism is all these meltdowns. Trying to process change or new things. Or even being told to do or not do something!

But I know its who I am and I'm not alone. There's so many of you out there who have these moments. This makes me feel better about myself. I am so sorry to my family who have to deal with me. I do feel sad about that as I never want to put my mum or any other family member though it, but they happen out of the blue I've even started to have meltdowns over food I didn't like or want.
And through all of these I've just been strong and found little things that managed to calm me down and I will say the salt lamp is great. And I hope the meltdowns get more easier as I get older to cope with.

Chapter 4

My Obsessions.

Through the years I've always seen things that have caught my eye. I get obsessed with them so quickly, like a song, a film or a TV programme. Songs are the worst thing for me though, I repeat songs for weeks even months, like I'm doing right now while I type this book. I have my headphones on, and the song is: "I Feel Alive" by We the Kings…check it out!

It will take me a while to stop listening to the same song over and over and move on to a new one!

Then there's films, mainly School of Rock that I got obsessed with. I watched it so many times, it's my all-time favourite film. I don't watch much TV I'd rather be writing a story and using my imagination.

But this film really did catch my eye as did my most favourite TV programme, Hannah Montana. This was something else I was hooked on. I watched it all the time and never shut up about it! I had all the CDs and the DVDs I couldn't stop watching it or listening to her songs. She was even in some of my stories just for fun, with myself meeting her. I just couldn't get this thing out of my head same as any songs. Whenever I went on caravan holidays it was always Hannah Montana with me. I even got the Hannah Montana wig and was wearing it when I went to my Grans which was funny! Her reaction seeing me with this blonde wig.

Now today I still collect Hannah Montana or even Miley Cyrus. It is a weird feeling when you get obsessed with something, not many people understand, they think you're crazy! My family were great about it though.

Now at this moment in time I'd say I'm a little obsessed with Mickey Mouse. I lost my Silly Grampa and it was our last conversation before he passed away. So, Mickey Mouse started to be something I had to have. My living room is now covered with Mickey Mouse. I feel like it helps me cope with his passing. It does make me super emotional though. Happy tears of his memory and sometimes sad because I miss him so much. I've always loved Disney just not as much as I love Mickey Mouse today. I even have 4 Mickey Mouse jumpers. Bags, shoes, hats, posters, canvas's and stickers and a rug!

I was playing a game when he was alive, a Disney one, and he noticed and asked Yeah that's how that chat started, best last conversation…ever!

I've also been obsessed with Justin Bieber in the past. His music mostly but I had his posters, his CDs, his DVD and a book. There was never a time I wasn't listening to his music I even took selfies with the poster I had of him which was on my door, so it felt like he was there in person! Another thing was skulls. I loved skulls on clothing, on bedding and more. Probably because as I said I always wanted to be a Rockstar so that probably links to that. I wore everything skulls and yeah, I had a skull bedroom I loved the Emo style. I felt cool, that's probably why I got so obsessed with skulls for a few years. Most of my obsessions last years. The Mickey mouse one as I wrote on the other page will be a forever. It is something that reminds me of my grampa but most only last years I calm down a bit with it but still love the music.

As I said on one of the other pages, I've always been obsessed with Avril Lavigne and her colours. She wore black and pink. My most favourite song of hers was Girlfriend. I played it all the time and used to dance to it everywhere. I had a cool pink limo on my 13th Birthday. I wore Pink and black had had her DVD as a gift. I had a blow-up guitar which was also those colours. I even had an electric guitar, I had it for Christmas off my dad, a pink one and it was awesome! I haven't got it now, just never had the time in the end to use it. There are so many things in my life that I've got obsessed with its hard to keep up with everything. No matter if anyone thinks your weird, you must always ignore them and keep doing what you love as long as you're not hurting yourself or anyone else.

Chapter 5

Being a Tomboy

Confused About My Gender.

I've always dressed as a boy. I wear boys clothing. I feel cool, I have never really been the girlie girl.

I wore a skull dress on my 18th birthday and on my 19th birthday, but apart from that I will probably never wear a dress ever again! It started around age 10 I didn't like being girlie. I even ended up with short hair on and off and through the years I've even been a little confused with who I was but apparently that's part of autism, being confused with your gender? It took a few more years to get comfortable with who I am. I just realised I can dress like a boy and still be a girl and enjoy being myself. I loved all the skull clothes and black jackets and jumpers, loved my black skinny jeans.

Especially when everyone around me was very girlie, like my cousins, and here's me! I never wore skirts, definitely not my thing. I did feel the odd one out, but at the same time I loved being myself. I sometimes said I was an Emo or a Goth but, in a boy, kinda way or as I kept saying a Rockstar but a boy looking one. I did feel amazing, it's good to feel like yourself even if nobody else likes it. That's probably why I couldn't walk in those high heels on Christmas time!

I have never worn make up or really done things to my hair, I just always wanted to look awesome. I used to wear Dr Marten boots, the black ones, and Skull bracelets and chains it was cool.

I say girls can wear boys' clothes and boys can wear girls' clothes and its ok as long as everyone is happy being themselves. It is a sad thought when some people don't understand why we dress the way we do but that's life.

Like today I have a boy's t-shirt and boys tracksuit bottoms on. I do wear Disney jumpers and tops as I love Disney, that's about as girlie as I will go but then again boys can wear Disney too, everyone can and that's ok. I've even got shirts here that I wear, I do love being myself, I love being boyish and dressing the way I do, it makes me happy being able to wear whatever I want, I never use handbags, only rucksacks.

There was even a time in my life that I felt I wanted to be a boy. I did question my sexuality. I wasn't happy being a girl everyone said its part of autism and at the time I didn't think it was.

I was fully sure I was not a girl and I spoke to a doctor. He said I had to live as a guy for 2 years. I think part of my sexuality was also a big issue with my gender as well not just part of autism.

I had always dressed as a boy and had short hair but that was part of me regardless. I am happy today living as I am, being a girl but dressing as a boy and I like my shorter hair. I'll never be a girlie girl, but I'll always love myself for who I am. I think everyone else should do the same and if anyone is confused about their gender you will figure out who you are boy or girl and be happy with yourself.

Chapter 6

School.

In school I remember being a small child and put on my own table, away from the other kids and not being able to concentrate. I was always fiddling with something, a pen or pencil. This was in primary school. I never could learn properly with so much going on in my mind. I couldn't write as well as the other kids and my drawings were kinda messy, but I was always the happy kid in school. I remember ending up on the smiley face chart, just to get me to focus, which did help a lot. In school concerts I would be the one standing there crying or biting my nails. I was shy and didn't want to join in with the other kids.

I think my favourite times at school were play time and toy day. I could just do my own thing and be comfortable. Getting older and going to comp was difficult. School was harder for me, I felt nervous and shy. I didn't make any friends and I found it harder to learn, maths I think was the hardest for me. I always had an LSA (learning support assistant) to help me, but I still struggled. Art and English were my favourite subjects as I was good at them. I started to do good drawings and I loved writing stories, that's how I always loved English while everyone else hated it and didn't want to write so much words. I always was the one to get excited. But then through the years of comp school I ended up in an STF where people with special needs go to get more support and help. Yeah that was great but then that's when the name calling started, names I don't even want to say in this book but let's just say they upset me, made me feel uncomfortable.

I did love school, the best part of it, apart from my favourite lessons was break time, getting to write my stories on the table. I hated the name calling which made me not want to be there. I would rather be home even though I didn't like being home because of all the past that happened. I can't forget P.E. This is another thing I hated at school especially on the cold days because I have got something called Raynaud's Disease. This is where my fingers and hands turn white and red, it is very very painful. I did sometimes say to teacher and once or twice I got to stand aside. The other thing was ball games! I was always terrified of being smacked in the face with a ball!

I felt silly and childish, but it was just part of my autism being scared of the ball.

Then there was this one girl who seemed to hate me and want to pick on me a lot. She made me feel nervous. She even got me into trouble a few times, saying I did horrible things to her when I didn't. I guess the one that's horrible to you always puts the blame on you. It was so frustrating, and nothing was really done about it, this is why people end up feeling so low and don't want to go to school when there's people who make it a horrible place to be. Things need to be done about it at the time. Bullying is never ok. I was already suffering from epilepsy at this point in my life. It had come back, and I had many fits in school that I had to be sent home. I don't think having people calling me names helped me as it made me stressed. There were lovely teachers though, I couldn't choose who my favourite teacher was as they were all nice. But there was only one teacher who didn't like me for some reason, or I felt she didn't like me. The rest were amazing which made me like school more.

Most of the other people didn't like me I felt. I was never the most popular girl in school which didn't bother me as I was happy with one or two friends. That was great as I've never wanted to be popular as I never liked too much of a crowd. Too many people in one room always made me feel nervous even does today. I don't like crowds, it makes me anxious, even now and I'm 26!

As I said this is where I met my first boyfriend, we had so much fun together. We are still good friends; I think about him a lot. I just don't talk to him any more like I used to as he's busy, I do miss him a lot.

My most scariest moment in school though was when I had to have an injection in my arm as I've always hated needles. I remember being the most scared I've ever been. I remember feeling faint, but I was ok and got it done. I was so relieved when it was over. Today a needle is fine (I have 15 tattoos!) I haven't had an injection for a long time, so I don't know how I react now. I was scared about fainting at the time but the teacher that was with me was great, she calmed me which is why I was probably so brave. Years later in my prom, I had to wear a bluey green dress and wear make up the most girlie I've ever been in my life! I felt ok up to the point where I got into the limo and I hate to say it as I do feel ashamed now, but I cried. I didn't like it and told my friend to ring my mam. When I got to the venue it was ok. There were loads of people which made me nervous, but it did end up as a good time.

At the end of comp, I was absolutely gutted. I received my report card. It said I had failed Art and English. The 2 things I did well at and really worked hard at all my school life. I guess we all struggle at school especially when we have special needs. My advice to you is make the most of it, try your best because before you know it you are an adult. If you are being bullied, shout it from the rooftops! Tell every adult in your life about it and try and stick up for yourself.

Chapter 7

How I Am With Food.

Throughout the years I've always been very fussy with foods. It can be because of the texture, the flavour or even the smell. As a kid I'd only eat chicken nuggets, chips, sausages and mash potatoes. That was about it! I never used to eat anything the family was eating. When they would have Chinese and I'd be eating a sausage with just chips, same as if we went to any restaurant of course I'd be the one being fussy.

My mam always tried to get me to eat other foods with everyone else and it would gross me out. I was never the type to try new things, even the look would put me off.

Even in school I'd be the one kid that didn't know what to eat as I didn't really like anything unless it was on my list of foods. Bright colours like green or red would instantly be a no! Everything was always yellow or brown. I would look at what my family were eating as I started growing up and wished I liked their food, but I definitely knew I wouldn't even try them.

It did annoy me for years, but I did enjoyed everything I was eating so that made me happy.

My mam knew she just had to let me eat what I wanted to; she knew she couldn't force me to eat other things. She always understood why, especially because I was a child and you can't force any child to eat something. When I became a teenager, my mam did start making me try more foods. As I got older and understood more. The worst was tomatoes, which didn't go down well at all as I started gagging. I didn't like how juicy it was and the texture, never again did I eat one of those! Another thing was cauliflower cheese, I said I will never eat or smell that ever again! There were many things I did try but just looking at most things grossed me. One day we were at Black pill park after doing a race and we went to the cafe. My mum had got tuna pasta and I decided to be brave and taste some and just out of the blue I love it and I felt proud!

Being Autistic food has always been a big issue for me with textures and flavours even the smell of food so trying tuna for the first time was amazing. It turned me into being brave with all sorts of foods after that. Like other fish and even garlic. I started trying more meats like proper chicken and beef. I went from being the worst fussy eater to then being a little adventurous. Today as an adult, I am still a little fussy. I don't like foods with bits in it, I have to always take the bits out before I eat it. I still don't eat very colourful foods like greens and reds, I don't like most vegetables and salads.

I have foods I can't stop eating because I love the flavour and the smell and that's garlic. I put that in all my foods nearly everything!

When I cook, I add garlic, I know your probably thinking how? Because a lot of autistic people hate the smell of garlic, a lot of people I've asked said they hate garlic, but I guess everyone is different. I know some people with autism who love salads and I don't. Then there's mayonnaise, I can't stop eating that with all foods and I even add garlic to it to make a garlic sauce. Some may say is horrible, but I think it's really good. With some pizzas, I have to take all bits off before I cook it. If it's got anything I don't like, that can take me forever and can be annoying. With bread that have seeds, I have to pick them out one by one until they are all out for me to eat it. With normal bread, I still take the crusts off even though it is just the bread and tastes the same I just don't like them.

I'll always be the same now with foods I think, but I am glad I'm not the fussy little girl I used to be.

Chapter 8

Sexuality

Through the years I've had a few boyfriends only one I could of said I loved. The rest I was not attracted to or didn't feel comfortable with. It felt very strange. I have had celebrity crushes that were girls and I didn't think anything of it just thought it was my mind acting weird. As I got older, I started to realise maybe I'm not into boys and I'm into girls. I did have my first girlfriend when I was 19 and it felt crazy but in a good way. When I came out to my mam, she was very accepting and wanted to tell everyone I was. I thought maybe she was gonna do a pride party for me because she was that understanding!

That's when I figured yeah, I'm definitely a lesbian but my mind still played games with me. I started being confused about who I was. I even thought I was a boy in a girl's body. I told everyone to call me Aiden, I thought I was a straight guy who was into girls. I said on the other pages I've always dressed like a boy.
My head was all over the place, I didn't know who I was, but I was happy no matter who I was as my family accepted me.

Years later I figured it all out, I'm definitely lesbian and I started to accept I was. All I want is to be happy being me. I started to have more crushes on girls older than me.

I joined a dating website which I didn't think I would do, I don't really like dating websites as I feel like not many people want to talk to you and when they do they end up going quiet! Maybe it's just me who knows. I have had girlfriends, 2 proper ones. One I was very much in love with it, but it just didn't work out, she didn't have feelings for me in the end. My very last girlfriend made me find myself. I knew then that I'm 100% lesbian because of how in love I was, it felt amazing. It was just a shame it didn't work out. People need to realise that someone who is autistic can fall in love too, just like anyone else. We have feelings like anyone else. We can have our hearts broken, we hurt, and we cry. It doesn't matter if we are autistic this proves we can all still fall in love with whoever, autism doesn't stop us, it may make it harder for us but will never stop us. Autism hasn't stopped me and I'm proud of my sexuality and always will be.

I think having autism and being lesbian really confused me. I thought my head was going to explode trying to find love with anyone, it's kinda hard for someone like me. But now it feels amazing to know my own mind and to know who I really am. To have such a supportive family around me to help me be who I am today. Whether you are a boy who loves boys or a girl that loves girls or even if you're bisexual it really doesn't matter…

LOVE IS LOVE!

Don't let anyone tell you different or bully you for it. There is only one race, the human race!

We live in a shocking world where we get bullied for being who we are and that needs to change!!

Chapter 9

Living On My Own.

For years I've always wanted to live on my own like any adult. When I was 18 almost 19 my social worker got me on the list for a coastal flat. I was on the list so long thinking no, it's never gonna happen for me, I'll never be able to live on my own.

Suddenly I heard back that there was definitely a flat available for me and it was quite overwhelming, but I was ready! After a while I came to see the flat it felt weird but so awesome. My stepdad Lee managed to get the keys quicker so my family could paint and get carpet down as it was empty. The family started decorating my flat and I brought bits and bobs too, some lovely pictures in frames to put in the kitchen and my mam took some photos of me at my home, and finally flat was all finished!

We brought a table and chairs, a sofa and it looked like a proper home, so cosy. My mum said bye to me and went home to her house. I got emotional, it felt weird being left on my own for the first time, in my own home and my mother leaving. I never thought I'd be living alone without my mam. I thought I'd always be living with her forever, I guess. The best thing about moving down here was living closer to my Nanny Bailey as she has a flat in the Marina. I started seeing her more with my Grampa Bailey as they live about 10 minuets away. I got my first pet, a budgie called Avril who sadly died from some sort of fit. I miss her so much on times, she was quite noisy! I always knew how to cook after watching family do it so that was easy for me, but I did have some pretty scary moments happen in my flat with food.

One time I put half a jacket potato in the microwave to cook thinking it be fine. It blew up and there were flames coming off it! I got so scared but knew what to do. I fanned it with a towel in the micro and it worked. I've burnt a few things, loads of bacon and I remember having the fire alarm go off trying to make it crispy and I don't like loud noises at all. But apart from that I think I've done ok. I don't put half potatoes in a microwave and I no longer try and make my bacon crispy!

Family would come and visit a lot which felt great and I have the best neighbour. This was a relief as my neighbour could have been anyone, luckily, I didn't have anyone that was too loud or mean or who didn't like me because of my autism. My neighbour likes me even though I think she got fed up of my letters as I always got shy and sent her letters to speak to her. I did this to my auntie Ali for a while just part of my autism, but we just talk instead now.

It's always been a quiet area. My town is only about 10 minuets away walking and its easy for me to do my shopping. I use the scan and shop, and this really helps me with my money, I can see how much I'm spending before I have to pay.

I've had a lot of great memories here.

Just because we are autistic doesn't mean we can't do these sorts of things. Even if it feels like it will never happen, years ago I didn't think it would until I got this flat. Even today it still doesn't feel real, but I know it is.

Today 8 years later I still live here. Now I have a Mickey Mouse living room, I'm more grown up than I was when I first moved in. A lot has happened, but it still feels great to be here. I've had fun sleepovers with my cousin Lewis, a few weekends my mam comes here. On Tuesdays my Nanny Bailey calls over. I love having visitors especially when its family as it can get a bit lonely but having Facebook to talk on helps. I cook more but I do have a lot of takeaways delivered. I love playing music and I do have Reborn dolls these are realistic dolls that people have which keep me company I just love their cuddles.

Chapter 10

How Reborn Dolls Help My Autism & Anxiety.

So, I have these dolls that are called
Reborns. They are dolls that are hand
made to look like real babies.
People have them for all different reasons
Maybe because they can't have real kids or because they
lost a baby or just to collect them. Sometimes it's to be
able to have a baby again. These dolls don't cry, poo or
grow up they stay little and quiet and I have a baby boy
called Cory. He comforts me when I have an autism
meltdown or when anxiety starts playing up. I have had
him for a year now. He has controlled my anxiety
attacks from quite bad to really mild just but cuddling
him. Some people don't agree with reborns, they call
them names which really upsets me, But I know they are
just being mean and have no understanding.
I would prefer if people asked questions and tried to
understand why I've got them instead of being mean.

I enjoy dressing Cory and pretending to feed him with a bottle. He has his own wardrobe and bouncer seat and clothes. I do love to cuddle him all the time it feels amazing. I've always wanted to be a mother to 5 children. For years I said I wanted 5 kids! I really want to be a mother. I did hope to be a real mam by the time I was 24 but it didn't happen. However, Cory helps me feel like a mammy so much. Some people don't understand this and think it's strange or creepy which does upset me, but I know that's just some. Most people love them and understand why I have them and how much they help. All I do when I have a meltdown is go and pick him up and cuddle him. Sometimes I cry and they calm me down. I take them to the doctors and to the dentist to help me not get too anxious.

I take him shopping with me in the pram. I do love spoiling him, everything I do with Cory I would do if he were real. I know a lot of autistic people have these for the same reason as I do. I'm on a reborn group where I share photos of my baby with everyone and they share their photos and it's lovely.

If I didn't have Reborns I'd probably still have bad anxiety and my meltdowns would be worse and harder for me to calm. I'm glad they are about for people like me.

Chapter 11

Sensitive to Smells.

Being autistic I am very sensitive to smells. Mostly very strong smells that make me gag and give me headaches like smoke, tumble dyer sheets & lavender. Some of these smells are normal to an ordinary person. I know a lot of people don't smell things as strong as I do which can be very annoying. I've had these smells on Reborns and baby clothes. Mainly smoke and Tumble dyer sheets as I buy a lot of things second hand. The smells to me are terrible and now I get nervous that these smells are on my Reborns or on any other items. Like I'll ask my mam sometimes to smell things because I can smell tumble dyer sheets on things, and she can't smell it. To her it smells really nice. I can smell things from a mile away sometimes and others won't be able to smell it.

Smells get to me very quickly and affect me easily to the point they take my breath away. I have to keep them away from me or my head does start hurting and yeah, it's very strange especially when nobody around you are affected by the same scents.

This is another thing I hate about having autism because I want to like a smell, but my brain is telling me no, I even start crying from the frustration. I want a new nose, a nose that doesn't hate nearly every smell. I suppose a lot of people don't like the smell of cigarette smoke but like the other smells. I hate I feel like I have issues with my nose. As I said on another page even cauliflower cheese! I don't like the smell of nuts and coffee, even tomatoes and I hate the smell of honey they all make me feel grossed out. I know I'm not alone as there are tons of other autistic people that are the same, that are sensitive to smells like me.

Chapter 12

Making Videos.

In 2009 I started making videos for
YouTube just for fun and for the
memories. I did it for years, just spoke
on camera and recoded my family,
it felt great. It was lovely to look back at
them as well. In 2012 I started
making videos of myself more, started
talking about my autism and my anxiety
and I realised how confident it made me
opening up on camera, so I kept
doing it. It felt good because I wanted
to help others like me and show them its
ok to be different. We are all unique,
I got to keep recording my family at the
same time especially when my sister Poppy was born.

It made me want to record a lot more, that meant I got to
talk more about
Myself. It really helped because I have

always been nervous and been shy, I even did a video of myself feeling very emotional just to show how emotional you can get so with autism because of things being on my mind I t was hard though to edit all the videos I made, to add an intro and cut anything out that wasn't supposed to be there. I didn't edit the ones of myself with real emotions, I wanted everyone to see that. Editing took hours, I always thought watching my favourite YouTubers that it looked easy to make a video, edit it and then upload but it is definitely not.

It is harder than it looks but it was always fun. I've done about 1,000 videos already. I don't upload on YouTube any more now because it's changed now, it isn't as good as it used to be. I still do videos for Facebook and I do still watch other YouTubers, I just don't upload any of my own videos. I can't believe how confident I am today for just picking up the camera and recording myself. There's a lot of things that help autism, but we are all different in our own little ways which means different activities will help different people. You have to find your own way and try things out.

My Goals for the future

1. Keep helping people with Autism
2. Find a nice Girlfriend
3. Keep writing books
4. Get a dog (Like my nanny used to have)
5. Became a mammy to a real baby
6. Go to America
7. Get married
8. Meet my Favourite YouTuber- KidBehindACamera & his family
9. See Miley Cyrus on tour
10. Help the homeless
11. Do more with my singing

Hope you enjoyed looking into my life and how I cope with my own autism!
I hope my goals happen I will update you on my Facebook page: AmiesbubbleofAutism

The end for now

Printed in Great Britain
by Amazon